# DEATH ON THE BRIGHTON ROAD

Jon Newman

David Western

This edition is limited to
300 signed and numbered
copies of which this is no.

250

First published 2017

By Thamesis Publications
3b Webber Street
London SE1 8PZ
www.thamesispublications.co.uk

ISBN    978-0-9927045-2-0

Cover Design and Images: David Western
Printed by Imprint Digital www.imprintdigital.net

# DEATH ON THE BRIGHTON ROAD

## JON NEWMAN

### &

## DAVID WESTERN

Thamesis

Jon Newman is a writer and archivist who works in and writes about London. He has previously published work on South London, black history and photography.
His most recent book, River Effra, South London's Secret Spine, 2016, was the first comprehensive history of a much-discussed and much-misunderstood river.

David Western studied at West Sussex College of Design before moving to London where he has since lived. He is an urban landscape artist who works from photographs and drawings to produce detailed paintings that document the changing faces of London's streets.

Acknowledgements
Thanks to all the Crowdfunder supporters and Arts Council England for their financial assistance in this publication.

# Preface

This is an account of a bike ride that I made in 2011 with the artist David Western. The text, illustrations and maps that we subsequently created as a response to the journey forms one part of a much larger London-wide work that we have been occupied with over the past eight years and which will shortly be published as From London Stone. This chapter, Death on the Brighton Road, is being published separately as a limited edition book to coincide with our exhibition Between Dog and Wolf, A South London Twilight held at Morley Gallery in June 2017.

 Among other things, Death on the Brighton Road is a nine mile ride, from the second mile stone to the eleventh, along the route of the old coach road: a sort of penal point-to-point which begins at the site of the former Surrey gallows on Kennington Common (the Tyburn of South London) and ends at the gallows and gibbet that used to stand at Smitham Bottom, passing three other execution sites along the way. It is also a journey down the A23 from St Mark's church at Kennington to a now derelict pub in South Croydon, through the suburbs of Brixton, Streatham and Thornton Heath.

The text was written in 2011 and six years on, enough has changed to turn it into a historical account in its own right. The notion of the streets of South London as fixed points feels increasingly precarious, superfluous even, as London ceases to be just a geographical space and turns instead into a real-time database of property futures whose rapid mutations even the ground-truthers struggle to stay abreast of. Some of those shifting points were already anticipated at the time of our journey: the Tesco's redevelopment in Streatham came to pass; the Half Moon at Broad Green is gone. The Red Deer at Smitham is now derelict and the August 2011 riots have further winnowed the street scape of North Croydon.

But none of these actual or hypothetical developments, not even that grimmest of regenerative whimsies rumoured in the reframing of Brixton Prison as a boutique hotel, can quite compete with the first and greatest act of forgetting and reinvention in which a former site of human execution could be recast 25 years later as a Christian church. Tyburn, London's other major gallows site at Marble Arch, has a convent shrine built over it specifically to remember its Catholic 'martyrs' hanged there. Kennington gallows by contrast has slipped away from view almost unacknowledged beneath the foundations of an Anglican church.

Jon Newman 2017

# DEATH ON THE BRIGHTON ROAD

❖

*"We whose ancestors were all hanged, why should we talk of ropes!"*

Thomas Carlyle, 1843

Dave texts me early one Friday evening. He is in the back of a car somewhere near Purley on the Brighton Road and appears to be undergoing a sort of twilight epiphany. "Extraordinary location we just went past, that vast playing field just south of Croydon, right on the edge. It's a great image". By the time I respond, he is out of signal, deep into Sussex along the A23. But he tells me later about the spectral cityscape he glimpsed from the rear window while heading south along the Purley Way: a darkening acreage of playing fields, the evening sun raking shadow-lines from the goal posts and the skyline pinnacles and flourishes of Croydon's boomtown, notched into silhouette as the lights begin to glow yellow in the towers.

I have a nagging feeling about the place he describes, of something previously glimpsed or once-read about. I can recall an image of a lonely common "south of Croydon called Smitham Bottom" where prize fighters would meet up before a crowd by a gallows; it was a coloured print I had once seen in a book, which showed two bent and labouring lumps of flesh in the foreground, behind them a wall of watching faces and then the backdrop of the hills. Set among the crowd, rising up above it like the emblem of the age, was the bracketed arm of the gallows. I go and check for its location on an old map, Rocque's 1762 map of Surrey, and find it just south of Croydon, at the eleven-milestone along what would become the Brighton Road. The map marks the symbol for the gallows just next to the milestone, at the junction with Sanderstead Lane. Dave's spectral vision of Croydon from the playing fields was further to the west along Purley Way; the future by-pass was still nothing more than open fields. It wasn't the same place.

1

Rocque's map is intriguing in the limited way it makes use of symbols. At the site of the prize fights at Smitham Bottom there were two: the milestone (M.S.) and the gallows (an inverted L with a pendant serif hanging down). How had he decided on the few important and recurrent landscape features which merited abbreviating down? Almost everything else on the map is drawn representationally: churches, houses, the contours of the hills, the very trees lining the edge of fields. Later mapmakers tend to reduce every aspect of existence into a symbol (Church with spire, Station (closed), Lighthouse (disused), Electricity transmission line), so it felt curious that Rocque had been able to make do with just these two, as if the measured mile and the hangman's noose were particularly significant markers of urban existence.

The coincidence of execution sites and mile markers was not accidental. Certainly by the eighteenth century these objects reflected linked aspects of social control and a shared anxiety about crime. They tended to be found in close proximity to criminal activity: the footpad loitering at the edge of town by the two-mile stone or the dark man on horseback in the lee of some low trees where the turnpike edged the common. Peter Linebaugh in his book The London Hanged describes the tension between "commercial society represented by turnpikes and the subsistence economy associated with waste, weald and common" as one part of the larger conflict

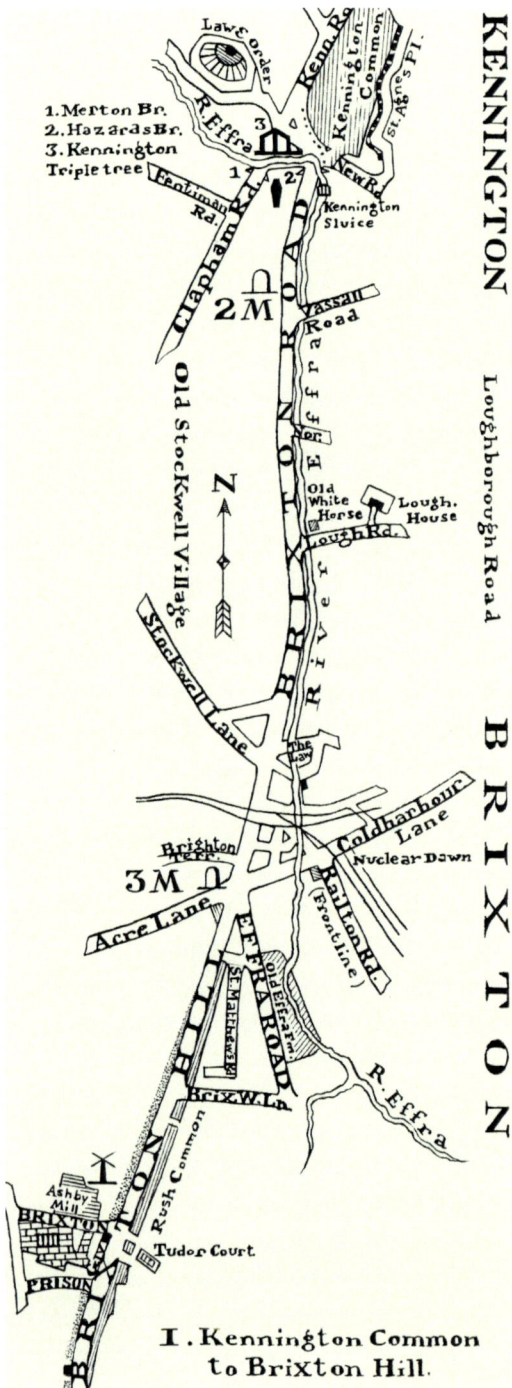

I . Kennington Common
to Brixton Hill.

2

between personal property and common rights.  Having turnpiked the highways, measured off the milestones and enclosed the commons, the gallows and gibbets could be slipped into the public spaces left in between.

The gallows at Smitham stood on common land by the eleven-mile stone. Back down the same highway towards London, just beyond the two-mile stone, another gallows was positioned at Kennington Common. And so a journey takes shape, a sort of carnal point-to-point along the Brighton Road between its execution sites. Dave and I arrange to meet at Kennington where Ogilby, in 1675, had warned coach travellers reading his road book that "you will pass as a landmark, a place of execution".

Kennington's gallows was on a triangle of waste ground at the point where two coach roads (now Brixton Road and Clapham Road) diverged beyond the common on their routes out of London. It stood on a low mound which rose gently on three sides and dropped away sharply to the west where the River Effra flowed beneath. It was clearly visible to passing travellers along both turnpike roads and easy for the London crowds of spectators to find. Kennington had its seasons, its hanging days always followed on from the Lenten and Summer Surrey assizes. In March or April the judgements would be given at Kingston court house from where the condemned carts would rattle along the valley to Kennington; in August the verdicts would be handed down at Croydon or Guilford and the prisoners in their tumbrils would labour slowly over the Surrey hills and along the coach road to the common.

There was always a good showing for these pageants of retribution and they brought out the evangelist preachers piggy-backing on the spectacle as well.  Charles Wesley and George Whitefield both came to Kennington, blinking in the sunshine and scenting a good crowd to lead in prayer.  Wesley came "and cried to multitudes upon multitudes, 'Repent ye and believe the Gospel'".  There is an

**DEATH ON THE BRIGHTON ROAD**

A road map in 4 sections showing the journeys to the edge of South London made by Jon Newman and David Western in March and June 2011 to research the execution sites, burial grounds and other curiosities between Kennington Common 2ᴏᴍ and Smitham Bottom 11ᴍ Also including : The mystery of the Whitgift Alms houses and the vision from Purley Way.

Drawn by
David Western
LONDON
MMXVII

| KEY | |
|---|---|
| 1 M | Milestone. from London stone |
| | Road, Path and relief. |
| | River. Road bridge. Rail. |
| | Heath Park and Common |
| | Farmland. |
| | Pond. |
| | Windmill. |
| | Site of execution |
| | Burial ground Cemetery. |
| | Church etc. |
| | Prison. Gaol |
| | P.H. Inn. |
| | Dead building |

engraving that shows Whitefield preaching before the Kennington gallows. Three corpses swing to the left of him. The spectators (the *mobile vulgus* standing and the wealthy seated in their coaches) wait with arms spread and eyes raised in thrall. A huckster is shouting in the foreground, "Hot pies, true confessions, body parts... everything must go". On busy days the condemned might be turned off five or six in a row and the relatives of the hanged would run forward to pull on their dancing legs to give them a quick end: 'Suss. per coll.' or 'dead of the hempen fever'. After they had been cut down, the rope burns on the necks of the dead would glow like the colour of an unripe blackberry.

Here came the unwashed of the Surrey-side, lured from their burrows on Three Coney Lane and from out the Borough by the wood-block-printed promises of the Flying Stationers and the Last-Dying-Speech men, their new-pressed leaves gripped tightly between ink-blackened fingers. The visceral pantomime of a High Treason execution with its promise of dismemberment needed extra soldiers to manage the crowd. When the Jacobite rebels Towneley and Fletcher were despatched here in 1746, the judge had ordered "while they were yet alive, their bowels should be taken out and burnt before their face". The stink of the spectators barely stifled the barbeque aroma.

Hither too flew the foragers of the battlefields, the eternal butcher birds: Huginn and Muninn, Odin's ravens, old Adam the carrion crow, 'heavy with marrow', the speckled kites of Maldon and the crows of Flodden field. Francois Villon's 'pies et corbeaux' followed the blood line from the Paris gallows of Montfaucon to circle Tyburn and fly across the Thames to Kennington to await their Lenten feast: five or six bodies strung up, the flesh eaten away and rotten:

*Vous nous voyez ci attachés cinq, six:*
*Quant de la chair que trop avons nourrie,*
*Elle est pieça devorée et pourrie,*
*Et nous, les os, devenons cendre et poudre*

(And we, the bones, becoming dust and ashes...)

John Badger of Camberwell Green was the last person to be hanged at Kennington in 1799. Tyburn had offered up the engraver William Wynn Ryland as its final soul, eleven years earlier. Both men were executed for forging bills. Like John Barleycorn "they tied him fast upon a cart, Like a rogue for forgerie".  When William Blake was a child, Ryland had been proposed as a possible drawing teacher for the young boy; after meeting him William had turned to his parents saying, "Father, I do not like the man's face; it looks as if he will live to be hanged."

After Ryland and Badger, executions remained public, but the gallows were relocated to purpose built gaols: Tyburn's executions went to Newgate in the City of London and Kennington's to the purpose-built Horsemonger Lane gaol near the Elephant and Castle. It was part of a growing desire for decorum and oversight, a movement too away from the unfenced and the uncontrollable to the greater security of walled spaces. The crowd management was easier in a gaol and the risk of a rescue en-route vanishingly small. It was a move too away from such customary practices as the Kennington hangman's demand on the way to the gallows for six shillings and eight pence from the prisoner for his 'services'. The deterrent effect of the spectacle was undiminished when seen high up on Horsemonger Gaol's "spacious lead-flat" roof from where the felons of Surrey would now be hanged. When a celebrity like John Thurtell – sports promoter, amateur boxer and gambler about town – killed a man over a gaming debt in 1824, a special stage had to be constructed for his hanging at Hertford gaol in anticipation of the massed crowds. London obliged "sending forth its swarms... in every imaginable species of low and vulgar vehicle" for the glimpse of John 'going to his long home'.

The same year that Thurtell was hanged, St Mark's church was built on the site of the  gallows. In digging its foundations, the labourers turned up a fragment of the gibbet, "a curious piece of iron, which probably was the swivel, attached to the head of the unfortunate criminal". It was sketched, engraved and published in the parish history as evidence for "the versatility of earthly affairs" whereby a place of human sacrifice might become an Anglican church. The suburban process now began in earnest: the Greek Revival elegance of St Mark's upstaged the hangman's scaffold and the

villa builders began to lay their brick lines along the roadway for its new congregants.

In its churchyard this early summer morning there are London planes and cherry trees shading green lawns. The headstones have long been tidied away and are ranged two-deep round the walls, "like chairs before a dance" as Elizabeth Bowen once saw it. Time and weather have been playful and a line or phrase is still legible in places – 'God moves in a mysterious way his wond...' Elsewhere language has dissolved and the chiselled tops of the grave stones have softened into grey outcrops with lichen greening their curves. Ash saplings, self-seeded among their once-tidy lines, have pushed the sequence awry with their twisted trunks. Around the side of the church where the white stonework of the neo-classical frontage cheapens to banded yellow brick, a bunch of drinkers - descendants of earlier execution crowds - have congregated with their Special Brew. One is in a wheelchair, the rest squat on the grass with their cans and rollups, waiting for the rain. They wave as we leave and raise us a toast.

We cycle on down the Brixton Road, through the remnants of its Regency builders' boom and by the little piece of Byzantium on the corner of Mowll Street that is Christchurch, past what was the Old White Horse and is now the Brixton Jamm and under Brixton's pair of high railway bridges where the markets spill out from Station Road and Electric Avenue, on past Matthew, porticoed and pillared like her Kennington sister, and up Brixton Hill whose tatters of Georgian ribbon trail between the 1930s apartment buildings and the ox-blood geometry of Olive Morris House. As we cycle on up the hill, its blocks of flats compete with their differing versions of twentieth century style: the New Queen Anne of Brixton Court, the flat roofs and curved glass of Dumbarton Court and the high gables of Tudor Court on the other side of Rush Common. Apparently, Dave tells me this as we labour by it on our way to the hill's brow, Nick Cave used to live there in the 1980s, listening

to the sounds coming through the floor below from flat 29 and injecting a little diamorphine-tinged polychrome into its black and white Tudor. "Fum the Fourth" now sells Tesco ready meals and The Telegraph, boarded up, awaits the jingle of Pentecostal tambourines. The old cinema, for long-times a camping shop, has become a pop-up bar.

Brixton Prison is set back discreetly from the road behind more domestic frontages. Its high walls built around the remains of an older "house of correction" can only be seen if we divert off to the right. The women waiting in line on Jebb Avenue to be searched and to pass through the barrier are here to visit their men-folk. Once the women were to be found on the inside - it was a female convict prison in the 1850s – then after a spell as a military prison it reverted to an enlarged civil prison in 1897, this time for male convicts.

In 1901 the prison had been fitted out with an execution shed for a gallows but there are no accounts of it ever being used. Instead Brixton seems to have turned into the ante-chamber for capital punishments that would be carried out in other places. The Indian nationalist Udal Singh was imprisoned on remand here in 1940 for murdering Michael O'Dwyer, the former Governor of Punjab, in revenge for his role in the 1919 Amritsar Massacre in India. 21 years after the event he had trailed his man to London and shot him at a meeting in Caxton Hall. Singh was held at Brixton during his trial but was taken to Pentonville Prison to be hanged.

William Joyce, "Lord Haw-Haw", was in Brixton too. His trial for High Treason in 1945 was because of the radio broadcasts that he had made from Germany during the war in support of Hitler. Captured and returned unwillingly from Berlin to his old territory (a succession of flats and rented rooms in Crystal Palace, street fighting during the 1924 North Lambeth election campaign, BUF marches and meetings – all part of a strain of home-grown South London fascism that would endure long after his death), once again Brixton served as the waiting room for a despatch that would be executed elsewhere. Joyce was hanged at Wandsworth Prison in January 1946.

There may have been no formal executions in Brixton but there were deaths here aplenty. The prison hosted the self-inflicted martyrdom of Terence MacSwiney in 1920. Poet, playwright, Irish nationalist and the Sinn Fein Lord Mayor of Cork during the Irish War of Independence, MacSwiney was arrested by the British for possession of "seditious materials" and after a military trial was imprisoned here. Refusing to recognise the jurisdiction of the court he went on hunger strike and died 73-days later. Other inmates have since found more prosaic yet speedy ways to kill themselves. By the 1980s the medical wards of Brixton's F wing were notorious: a psychotropic bedlam within which a succession of damaged and frightened young men struggled for the exit between knotted prison bedsheets.

Now we are back on the route south where, beyond the prison walls just at the crest of the hill by Morrish Road, stood the five-mile stone. It was here in 1723 that a footpad, "Jack Gutteridge", ambushed a travelling cart, stuck a pistol in the driver's mouth and then blew the man's face off. He was hanged at Kennington the following year for his crime but his body was brought back here to be hung in chain on a gibbet in order to mark the site of his particular atrocity. The bodies of other felons hanged at Kennington would be displayed on the same gibbet in later years but Gutteridge was the first and his especial notoriety endured so that the spot was only ever known as 'Jack Gutteridge's Gate'.

Its location at the summit of Brixton Hill is tantalising in the way that it links back to a much earlier association. For here too, predating the five mile stone, had stood the 'Brixi-stan', an Anglo Saxon land marker which went on to give its name to Brixton Hundred, one of the ancient administrative sub-divisions of the county of Surrey. Brixton as a suburb is the relatively recent creation of the suburban builder and was never a historic place of settlement. Instead the summit of Brixton Hill provided an empty but visible geographical mid-point around which a number of parishes could conveniently be grouped. In pre-medieval time the 'stan' would probably have been the location for the meetings of its hundredal court. Elsewhere at other identified hundredal meeting places there is a strong correlation with archaeological finds of Anglo-Saxon execution burials and the siting of medieval gallows. No such evidence has yet been uncovered on Brixton Hill for such executions and burials, but it remains a likely location for such. So did an unconscious trace memory of Brixi-stan's earlier history and purpose also inform the siting of Gutteridge's gibbet? As we cross over the South Circular opposite the Crown and Sceptre there is a ghost bike, painted white and chained up to the railings as a fleeting memorial to the victim of a later "more random" execution.

The architecture becomes younger as we move on out. Despite all the demolitions and interjections Brixton Road still has a sense of itself as a Regency suburb; Brixton Hill is more confused; Streatham is late-Victorian bleeding into Edwardian.

II . Brixton Hill to Northwood Brook

Descending the brick-faced canyon of its High Road on a bike is a passage engineered with danger and any notion of lingering along the road-way has been severely discouraged. Back in Brixton, the stoners, the insane and the megaphone evangelists were ambling across the centre of the road by the markets and shouting at the cars, but here the weight of traffic and the central barrier – crossable only at the gaps between the railings and the fortified wall of planting - deter all but the self-sacrificial. As a townscape, its signatures are flatness and height; the stuck on frontages have little or no depth and there is a uniformity of street line with no niches or refuge. At the corners of each side turning "off of this high High Road" stand yet taller and more ornamental buildings, topped off with wedding cake pillars and arcaded onion domes. They feel like stage-set gateways that might just open on to glimpses of the

Orient – an expectation that quickly falters as the eye drops from their faience heights to the bright plastic fascias of the chicken joints and sari shops beneath. As we cycle on past and glance down, their vistas offer nothing more magical than repeating terraces of Edwardian red-brick decency marching tidily away.

Further along the High Road we pause opposite a triptych

of buildings: the old ice rink, mauve and pink at the front, peeling to an off-white along its sides; a carpet warehouse with its multi-coloured rolls like giant sticks of sugar candy; and between them Streatham's derelict baths and assembly rooms – its municipal grandeur masked behind block-boarded eyes and a padlocked and pillared mouth that can neither see nor speak of evil. The three of them have that numb and condemned look. The local historians and heritage organisations have been casting dice for their clothes: competing for fragments of stained glass, pleading for foundation stones to be reincorporated in the wall of the new car park. A local antiquarian has already secreted one memorial plaque in his front garden and it is whispered that the rink's ice making machinery may go to the Science Museum. Tesco, the twenty first century hangman, awaits the completion of these scrabbled obsequies and payment for his services.

Dave is scowling at the view from across the road, camera fallen awry in one hand, fag in the other. The light has gone and the grey pall behind the sad frontages will not speak to him. He insists that we wait for the sky to change. The buses and traffic grind by un-noticing as he paces, mutters, turns and faces back, waiting for a Turner or a David Cox to lean across and vein the banked cloud with their gold and cornelian pencils. Finally something creaks open and the space fills briefly with light. He kills the cigarette, screws the camera to his eye, half crouching as he shoots, recalibrates and shoots again, trying to pin the shadow lines.

Edward Thomas who cycled this road out to the North Downs before the First World War always enjoyed this part of the ride as he crested the "green dome" of Streatham Common. After the unbroken frontages of the High

Old Streatham High Road as seen in June 2011
and drawn by David Western in sections 2011
2017... 1. 1. church hall. b.190... d.2012. 2. Streatham Ice Rink. b.1931. d.2012. 3. Streatham
Assembly Hall and Baths. b.1927. d.20... 4. House
of the Hanted man. 5. Piscani Carpets/Car Wash.

Road, it feels like the gap-tooth in a brick mouth, a green space to poke your tongue into. Streatham was long the favoured retreat of grocers and brewers. Henry Tate settled here with his sugar millions, Henry Thrale a century before him with his beer money (his beer-belly of an outsize coffin still rests in St Leonard's crypt). In 1763 Samuel Beaton had stopped Thrale while he was in his coach travelling to Streatham and robbed him; he was hanged at Kennington for his trouble.

I think of the novelist R. S. Surtees whenever I pass over the common and of the time, in Jorrock's Jaunts and Jollities, when John Jorrocks rode out here for a day's paltry shooting with Nosey Browne. Nosey had recently withdrawn from the grocery trade in Southwark to a new-built villa on Streatham Common. His newly built 'Rosalinda Castle' was a masterpiece of scatter-gun faute de goût with 'fiery red-brick' castellations, loopholes and pea green casements around the Gothic oak-painted windows. He had a topiary holly bush trimmed to the shape of a fox, two wooden cannon on the battlements guarding a brace of chimney pots, a fish pond the size of a soup basin, an arbour overlooking a dung heap and an oyster shell temple for his carrier pigeons. Nosey's Streatham feels like an outlier for Wemmick's house in Walworth in Great Expectations but without the affection. Surtees has laid barbed wire around its edges and mined its vulgarities. The mistake is to dismiss him as a mere writer of 'huntin' and shootin'; he is more interesting than that. He was one of the first to write of the tawdry spaces at the city's edge where Victorian London bled into country: Soapy Sponge hanging about the Edgware Road at the end of the omnibus line; the demi-mondaines who once rode side saddle in the cheaper South London theatres ('hippodramas' at Astleys, pantomimes at the Surrey) but were now to be found hunting for husbands and riding to hounds at country house weekends; and of the interminable waits at railway junctions for the connecting train to the next meet. His writing catches an accelerating emptiness within Victorian society in its search for a meaning through the mindless pursuit of sport. He knew and he skewered the world of the hobbyist,

the sporting obsessive and the man who must have the right labels on his clothes.

Back on the London Road, travelling south through the longeurs of Norbury, we come to Thornton Heath and pause there to pick our way across the traffic to a curious sunken garden in the middle of its large roundabout. There is something fine and unexpected about coming upon bird song, yellow forsythia and young green birch in the heart of a busy road junction and we step down into its qualified calm. It feels a tentative space, not yet quite park, no longer mere roundabout. The abandoned public art in one corner might once have been a water fountain, its wooden benches encourage you to linger while the traffic circling above and around you has the opposite effect. A green triple-tubed stink pipe, only partly hidden by a flowering hedge, trumpets above what was once the old goose pond but which has since been drained and transformed into a sunken grove. But then as Sophie who lives here and knows it, says, "If it was still a pond someone would only piss in it". Upstairs on the highway, the rebuilt Horseshoe pub marks the start of Purley Way, laid in the 1930s to skirt Croydon and take the motorist on to Brighton, Croydon Airport and to Dave's

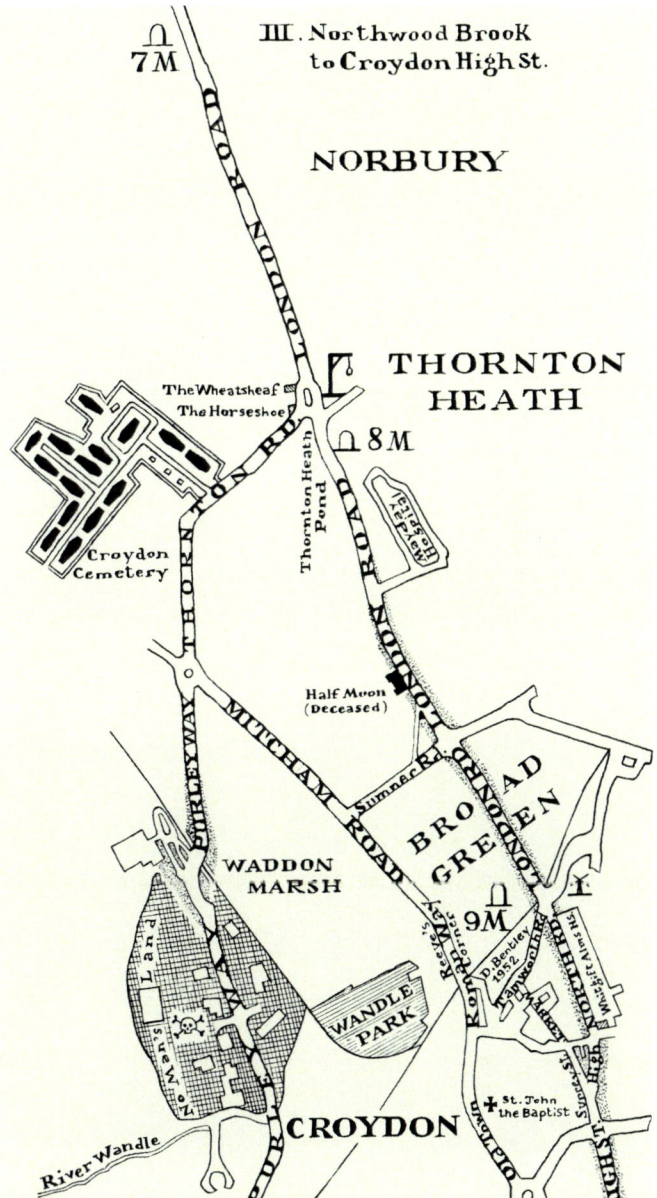

15

twilit playing fields. Its angled faux-Tudor gables are the first hint of the 'By-Pass Variegated' that awaits the traveller further along the Brighton Road with its road houses, filling stations and golf club pavilions running all the way to the coast. Dave climbs back out and crosses the lanes of traffic to a baker's shop to buy lunch while I sit in the sun.

Only later do I discover that the submerged space into which we stumbled at Thornton Heath had also served as a road-side place of execution. Later, when I check back on our route against Roque's map, I spot the tell-tale gallows symbol just above the eight-mile stone, at what was then the crossroads and is now the roundabout. It felt odd that I had missed this the first time I had looked at the map and then odder still that we had stopped here by chance for our lunch. Once realised, the history of the Thornton Heath gallows was soon uncovered. Variously known as Hangman's Acre or Gallows Green, enthusiastic bouts of public executions, mainly of highwaymen, took place here: six were hanged in 1722, another four in 1723. The keepers of the Croydon parish burial registers took a vicarious delight in itemising the particular fate of the remains of their executed dead. For William Hurley, hanged for murder in 1753, the register entry notes that, "his body given to the surgeons to be anatomised".

By the 1750s the proliferation of crimes that could be punished as capital offences had turned execution by hanging, despite its awe-full-ness for the individual sentenced, into a commonplace. If you could be hanged as easily for the theft of a pocket watch or a handkerchief as you could for rape or murder, then where was any sense of relativity? How was the state to demonstrate that certain crimes were to be regarded as more evil? The solution was the 1752 Act "for better preventing the horrid crime of murder" – quickly shortened to "The Murder Act" - which sought to create "some further terror and peculiar mark of infamy" over and above the mere action of capital punishment. One of these new statutory terrors was to be the anatomisation that William Hurley's body was subjected to after he was hanged at Thornton Heath.

Dissection of the hanged was not in itself new. Surgeons' assistants regularly attended Tyburn and Kennington to haggle with relatives for the bodies of the dead. This was one of the very few sources of fresh

16

human cadavers that could be easily obtained for surgeons to practise on. Two things changed with the Murder Act. Now the involvement of the surgeon was legitimate and approved, where previously it had been ambiguous and merely tolerated. The shift came with the stipulation that these dissections should now be a form of public theatre. 'Penal anatomy' was a deliberate humiliation to be carried out beyond, indeed instead of, the grave. Hurley was an early victim, the Act had only been in place for one year when he was executed, and I wondered whether it had been some sharp-elbowed local barber surgeon who had that trophy carried back to his Croydon rooms or whether Hurley's body had gone to London, like Richard West, hanged here in 1722 and "taken from the Thornton Heath gallows by the surgeons and carried to St Thomas Hospital".

These public dissections became crowd-pleasers. When a celebrity like John Thurtell was hanged at Hertford Gaol in 1824 the fascination was such that his body ended up in the anatomy theatre at Barts Hospital in London rather than remaining in the provinces. As the surgeon, Abernethy, cut him open crowds queued at a turnstile for tickets for a sight of his corpse "remarkable for its muscularity and symmetry". They peered into the pinned-back flaps of his chest at his un-caged organs, and scanned his viscera for the touch of evil. Thomas Rowlandson was there and turned out a quick watercolour sketch of the scene before the makers of death masks and the phrenologists started jostling for precedence: to purchase the rights to his face; or to finger the bumps and contusions of his skull to identify the mythical 'organ of destructiveness'. Once he had been picked over and harvested, Thurtell was 'converted into skeleton' and sent back to

Hertford. A face cast and a few of his pickled body fragments found their way into an Oxford Street shop window while a wax effigy graced Madame Tussaud's. But for Thurtell the supreme posthumous carnal tribute was to be the production of a de-luxe edition of his published trial notes, bound in his own lightly tanned skin. Thus it was for the A-listers, but of a South London side-show like William Hurley and concerning his judicial disarticulation at Thornton Heath, there is not a trace.

We finish our chicken rolls and get back on the bikes. As we cycle on, I am looking out for the eight-mile stone. It was one of the thirteen along this stretch of the road subscribed for by the inhabitants of Croydon back in 1743, and would have signposted the way for those out-of-town voyeurs coming in search of Hurley's execution at Thornton Heath. It has been dug up long-since and in its place the street furniture of the twenty first century is found at a density and complexity beyond mapping or cartographic symbols: road traffic signs, street names, warnings, CCTV camera posts, parking payment machines, 'No Street Drinking' signs. Cycling on down the London Road towards Broad Green, we pass Iris and Christine's flower shop, 'Floral tributes a speciality', and then a mushroom crop of white satellite dishes which have spored above the shop frontages and which are all pointing south to the towers of Croydon.

On the way to them we pass by the Half Moon in full wane. Buddleia adorns its fracturing pediment and through an upper window a bare brick wall is back-lit by the sky. The painted gilt of the sign for the "Lounge Entrance" tarnishes in the air. The Council's planners have judged and passed by on the other side. "A significant part of the roof is missing as are numerous windows. As a consequence any architectural merit the building once possessed

has been lost". Next door at the London Road Hand Car Wash, life busies on and a jerk chicken vendor has shoe-horned his caravan into the space in between. Beyond them, a once-tall gothic spire drowns in the shade of an office block, the faithful gather beneath a dome of gilded fibreglass for Friday prayers and the May Day ambulances siren their way back to the re-branded Croydon University Hospital.

Passing under the railway bridge at West Croydon station, Dave points down Tamworth Road on the right where, he says, Christopher Craig and Derek Bentley got disturbed while trying to burgle a confectionery warehouse in 1952. Craig had a revolver and he shot and killed Sidney Miles, the policeman who discovered them during the break in.

Because Craig was under age he could not be given a capital sentence and so it was the eighteen year old Bentley who was tried for the murder as a 'joint enterprise' and who was hanged at Wandsworth the following year as an example. Prompted by a 40 year campaign to have the case re-examined, initiated by Bentley's parents and continued by his sister, the long slow agonising about what Bentley might have meant when he shouted "Let him have it, Chris" (the gun or a bullet?), never mind the fact that he had not himself fired the shot, led in the 1990s first to a posthumous pardon and then finally to the quashing of his conviction.

Wheeling our bikes through its pedestrianized streets between the preachers and the buskers and the shoppers, Croydon offers us up the reek of retail: a lushness of perfumed soap, gusts of fast-food trans-fats and the burnt aroma of franchised coffee. Then, improbably, the Whitgift alms houses present themselves on a corner. Gloriously misplaced – except of

course that they were here first – they clutter up the corporate retail vision with their out-of-kilter street lines and elegantly understated Tudor brickwork. Above one of the gable ends the founders initials "I  W" are picked out in a darker colour:  John Whitgift, latterly Archbishop of Canterbury. Their unassailable heritage status is comparatively recent. Croydon borough and Croydon Tramways had tried for years to demolish them. In 1914 their buildings were felt to 'occupy a slightly obstructive position from a tramway and modern municipal points of view' and the 'many determined efforts to pull them down' only ceased in 1923.  In the 1890s Harper, the author of The Brighton Road, found Whitgift's brick initials "strange and reverent amid the shop signs of a latter-day commerce" - to which one can only weakly suggest that he really hadn't seen anything yet.

Alders department store next door has angled its frontage outwards to align with the Whitgift's older street line and, second-time around, Croydon's tram builders have acknowledged the alms houses with a grudging curve along the line of George Street. The mannequins modelling Alders' summer hat collection in their first floor window look down askance. Outside a Muslim scholar stands statue waiting for the bus. Our bikes clutter the passage of a big woman, double buggy the width of her hips, as she forges down towards Surrey Street market sucking her teeth and cursing at us for delaying her.

The road running south out of Croydon takes us under the aspirational inner-urban motorway of this wanna-be city and out into a long valley. To each side and beyond its ribbon of villas with the smaller streets climbing off of it you can see tree-capped ridges of the hills. There is a restlessness down below, a feeling of passage through and of moving along, the unthinkingness of elsewhere and the flash and flourish of passing trade (of Lahore curry, Turkish mobile phones, a Kurdish barber). It is the old 'open road' that has been widened, worn away, built back and resurfaced a thousand times. Stone carriers have filled pot holes and sweating navvies have raked the macadam. My grandfather and his brother used to pace along here on their night walks in the summers before the First World War, on their way from Gospel Oak to Brighton for the bank-holiday weekend. Edward Thomas may even have overtaken them on his bicycle. He paused here by Haling Park (where the Archbishops relocated their palace after Croydon's town centre became too pressing for them) to observe that "the long low green slope of the park, the rookery elms on it, the chestnuts above it above the roadside fence, are among the pleasant things which the besieging streets have made pleasanter."

Now we are beyond Haling Park and cycling down an arrow-straight highway with a prospect of yet higher hills rising before us. The street lamp standards semaphore down the line of the valley like gallows' arms, directing us to a strange hybrid building at the junction ahead. Half gin-palace, half road house, it has a mournful concrete deer, the colour of ox blood set high on its frontage among its stick-on architectural ornament and it is staring back up the road to Croydon. This is the Red Deer pub which stood beside the Smitham Bottom gallows. The Prince of Wales came to watch "Gentleman" Jackson defeat Fewterell in a prize fight here in 1788. Previously in 1749, James Cooper, alias 'the Butcher', had been executed and hung in chains at this spot. Cooper had shot Robert Saxby "in the lane leading from Croydon Turnpike towards Sanderstead" and his combination gallows and gibbet was set up at the road junction just by the eleven-mile stone to mark the site of the murder.

Gibbeting, also known as 'hanging in chains', was the second of the deterrents created by the Murder Act. As an alternative to anatomisation (not that the recipient had any choice) the judge could stipulate that a murderer's executed corpse be displayed on a gibbet. Public anatomisation was something of a one-off, the crowds came on the day and the bony remains were then confined to private collections like those of the Royal College of Surgeons. By contrast gibbeting was highly visible, surprisingly enduring and, in a Mikado-esque sort of way, allowed the punishment to both fit and map the crime. Murders committed along the public highway could now offer the pleasing retributive symmetry of having the criminal's body grace the same spot. Robbers of mail coaches and assassins of the turnpike (like Cooper or the two footpads on the Portsmouth Road at Kingston in 1787 who were "executed near the spot where the fact was committed and their bodies to be hanged in chains") were to become the unwitting conceptualists of their own site-specific installations.

It was a kind of travelling theatre. Sites like Smitham Bottom, where a one-off gallows segued into a semi-permanent gibbet, were visible roadside landmarks that aged and matured and stayed in the mind far longer than the twice-yearly hangings at fixed execution sites. The gallows at Kennington might draw their crowds on the day, but once the bodies had been cut down everyone went home. By contrast, along the turnpike roads out of London, clusters of richly didactic corpses could be found suspended in every instructive stage of putrefaction and decay.

IV. Duppas Hill to Purley.

There was a third and final horror tucked away like a sheathed sting in the tail of the Murder Act: the sting not of death itself but of the denial of burial, implicit in both anatomisation and gibbeting, and it was into this denial that the 'peculiar terror' of the Act was most intensely distilled. The residues of public dissections remained the property of the institution carrying them out: the viscera in saline jars at Barts Hospital and the

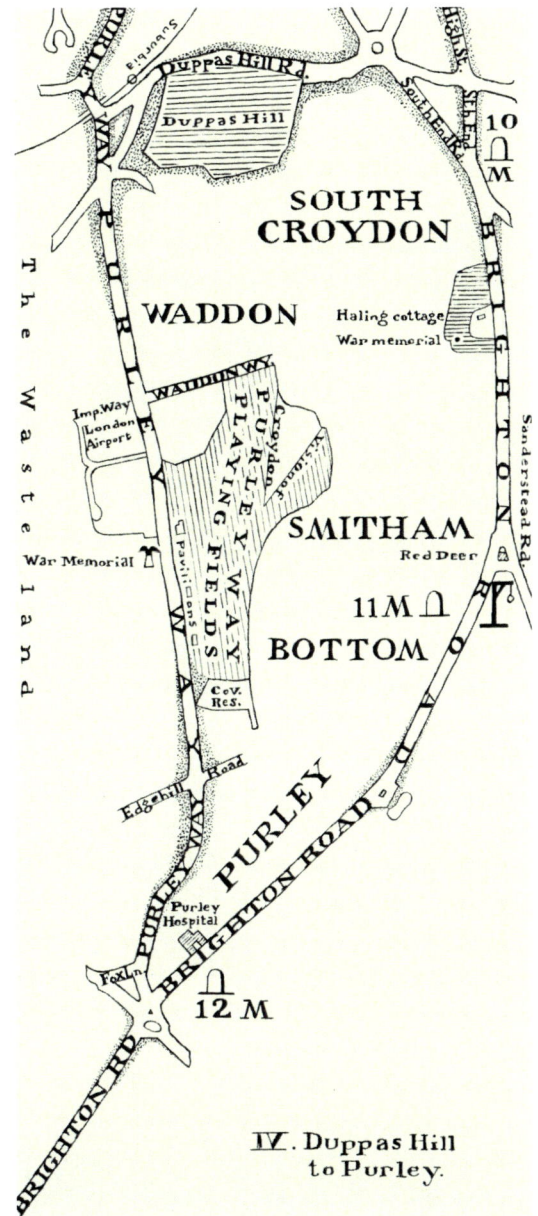

skeletons in the closets of the Royal College of Surgeons became a part of the institutional archive. In its way the gibbet was a property too, a form of enclosure and ownership. The corpse's skull would be trepanned and a swivel screwed into the top of the bone so that the body could be suspended from it within the gibbet's riveted iron cage. This was in turn locked and secured to a post. These intricacies of incarceration were to prevent the family from retrieving the body for burial. Additionally anyone caught attempting to remove and bury such remains laid themselves open to transportation for seven years under the Murder Act. Instead they were required to witness its slow falling away until just the top of skull remained secured to the rusting swivel.

The very precise 'infamy' entailed in the denial of Christian burial lay in the way that it challenged a profound taboo. Not only would it mean temporal disgrace for the family of the felon, but there would have been a widely-shared understanding of the spiritual punishment that this denial would involve: the victim's soul would never be at peace until his or her remains were gathered up into sanctified ground. The eternal limbo proposed by the Act, whether as a surgical specimen or as a pile of decaying organic matter by the side of the road, was a viciously effective extension of the social and religious stigma that was already imposed on suicides whose bodies were not permitted burial in consecrated ground.

Looking through newspaper accounts of sentencing under the Murder Act, I found myself wondering if some English assize judges had been reading Francois Villon's poetry in the original French. The press report of one sentencing at Exeter, which came out some 90 years before Swinburne published his English translation, echoes the particular horror of bodily dissolution that Villon described in his Epitaphe en forme de Ballade, also known as The Ballad of the Hanged. It was a poem he wrote in prison in anticipation of the very event (but from which he was then pardoned) and in it he imagines himself and his companions already dead on the gallows, enduring the flocks of magpies and crows that will peck out the eye sockets and rip away the beard and eyebrows from their rain-sluiced and sun-blackened corpses.

*La pluie nous a bués et lavs*
*Et le soleil desseches et noircis:*
*Pies, courbeaux, nous ont les yeux cavés,*
*Et arraché la barbe et les sourcils....*

Almost paraphrasing Villon's description of a slow decay

foreseen, the Devon judge sentenced the two men before him in 1788 to be hanged in chains "till the fowls of the air and the vicissitudes of the seasons have totally devoured and dissipated them".

No clue was ever offered at point of sentencing as to how long the devouring and dissipation might take, but it often proved to be a slow process. Jerrry Abershaw was tried at Croydon assize in July 1795 and sentenced to hang on Kennington Common. He processed in his tumbril from Croydon court house across Streatham Common and back down Brixton Hill 'entirely unconcerned, a flower in his mouth, his bosom thrown open... laughing and nodding to acquaintances in the crowd'. Like Jonathan Swift's 'Clever Tom Clinch' and William Hogarth's Tom Idle, the soon-to-be-hanged often

commanded an intense but brief celebrity. After execution Abershaw's body was cut down and carted to Wimbledon Common – the scene of his crimes along the Portsmouth Road – there to be hanged in chains. For the rest of that summer, "thousands of the London populace passed their Sundays near the spot as if consecrated by the remains of a hero". Three years later when Prime Minister, William Pitt, after slighting an opposition MP, George Tierney, was required to fight a duel on the common, Gillray's cartoon of the event has Abershaw's gibbet in the background like a named landscape feature. When Belcher and Gamble staged a prize fight there in December 1800 and again when Elias the Jew fought Tom "Paddington" Jones at the same spot a year later there was still enough of him left despite the devouring and dissipation for the printed handbills to use him as a signpost to the ring - "in the hollow near the gibbet of that extraordinary character Jerry Abershaw". The fresh-faced souvenir hunters and the picnicking amateurs of the summer of 1795 had contented themselves with filching the buttons from his coat, but the cognoscenti bided their time, returning in later years like magpies to slip their hands through his rusting cage

and snatch "from his decaying and piece-meal carcass the bones of his fingers and toes to convert into stoppers for their tobacco-pipes". What little was left of Jerry still turned in the breeze like Villon's dead companions, "Puis ça, puis là, comme le vent varie".

Abershaw was just a common criminal but for those executed for High Treason, like the Jacobite rebels despatched at Kennington in 1746, there was an additional political requirement for their bodies to endure as a memento perfidiae. After Francis Towneley and George Fletcher had been disembowelled, emasculated, dismembered and beheaded their heads were transported to Temple Bar in the City of London to be displayed on poles. Townley and Fletcher were the last to endure the pantomime barbarity of the full sentence of High Treason (quartering and emasculation ceased after their executions). Once decapitated, their heads were then par-boiled and coated in tar to extend their useful life. "I well remember", wrote the poet Samuel Rogers, recalling Townley's head on Temple Bar as a young boy 30 years after the event, when he would pass under its "black shapeless lump... Another [Fletcher's] pole was bare, the head having dropt from it."

Public executions became highly ritualised events and the final drink for those about to die (gin or beer for the men, something softer for the ladies) was soon institutionalised. Mary Edmondson was brought by post-chaise from her cell at Kingston to her execution in 1759 and "arriving at the Peacock in Kennington Lane before nine o'clock there drank a glass of wine" before being put in the cart and taken onto the common. James Randall preferred the Horns Tavern on the very edge of the common where "he begged leave of the officers to allow him to have some refreshment." Each place of execution had its neighbouring hostelries ready to do the last honours. On their way to Tyburn the tumbrils would pause at the Bowl Inn at St Giles; those set for Execution Dock gagged on their gin in the Turks Head in Wapping. Back at Thornton Heath crossroads it was the Wheatsheaf. Now we are come to Smitham Bottom, so we lock up the bikes and step into the Red Deer.

In the cavernous ballroom at the back of the pub the 'Private Party' signs are gathering dust as Cliff Richard and Paul Anka squabble for juke box air-time. Beneath the spreading tobacco brown stain of the front bar's ceiling, a machine on the counter vends sweets, toothbrushes, and lollipops. The two men playing pool apologise that there is no one behind the bar, "Oh, she's on her own today... she'll be out in a minute." A joyless woman eventually steps into view. No, there is no draught bitter today, nor is there any food. We take our lager and crisps and sit outside on the stone flags where the gibbet once stood. Buses grind by on their way to Purley on the one side; a modest terrace of houses point along the lane to Sanderstead on the other, the spot where James 'the Butcher' Cooper shot Robert Saxby in 1749.

We go inside when it starts raining. Back in the bar, the cadaverous gloom of the room has somehow increased and a funereal schmaltz is oozing from the music speakers. The figures on their stools seem to have stooped and set themselves into an ochre still-life. Then a

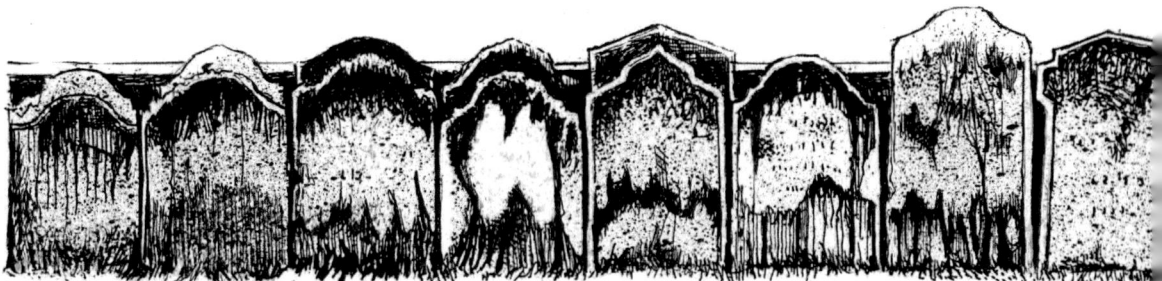

Glasgow drunk, Barnardine from Vienna by way of the Red Road flats, weaves across to us from the table, pool cue in hand, to elaborate one more time to the strangers his party trick: the time he once took the white off five cushions to get out of a snooker. He sets up the ball and places the chalk on the baize to demonstrate the near-impossibility of his position. We smile encouragingly but his first attempt sends the ball straight into the pocket and he collapses theatrically on the table. He tries again, the ball thuddingly obliges its way around the cushions and drops into the pocket. We applaud politely as he heads to the bar for another pint, "To help me get to sleep this afternoon".

Rocque published his map of Surrey in 1762 just ten years after the Murder Act's decaying by-products began to be displayed systematically along the high roads into London. So was his emphasis in marking gallows and gibbets at the expense of other features more than accidental, almost political? Was it an advertisement for deterrence through horror? Coach travellers planning journeys along the Portsmouth or the Brighton roads could run their finger down the engraved line of his map past the symbols for the gallows and gibbets and anticipate the falling scarecrow figures they would encounter along the way. They would have got the subtext too, that such sites were both the scenes of past crimes and also the lonely spots where the yet-unexecuted might await them still.

As gibbets and gallows became almost prosaic landscape features so representations of them increased. In addition to maps and road books they pervaded all sorts of other 'literature'. Their inky logos were on the tops of the discarded handbills of 'dying confessions' that could be found blowing around Tyburn and Kennington after hanging days. They were an ever-present allusion in Hogarth's brick-edged London prints, nudging and winking from street corners disguised as pub signs, street lamp arms and shop sign brackets. In his series of prints The Idle and Industrious Apprentices, the gallows is foreshadowed in the shape

of the looms at which Tom Idle works while its noose can be seen in the mooring ropes dangling from the boat that takes him down the Thames to prison. It is the same crowds and the same soldiers who turn out for Frank Goodchild's Lord Mayor's show as go on to attend Tom Idle's hanging. Hogarth could always see the skull beneath the periwig.

Gillray's engraving of Pitt's duel on Wimbledon Common showed Jerry Abershaw's gibbet just as his earlier print of the prize fight at Smitham Bottom when Jackson fought Fewterell in 1788 shows James Cooper's gallows poking through the crowd. Gillray returned to Smitham four years later to make an etching of Daniel Mendoza defeating William Ward at the same spot. This cross-over between public executions and prize fighting was particularly intriguing and had in a way triggered our journey down the Brighton Road. When Joshua Wheeler was hanged at Kennington for murder in April 1797 his printed 'last dying speech' reported that he was a "companion to the famous boxer Johnson", almost as if this was only to be expected.

Prize fighting, technically illegal but widely tolerated, had established its illicit spaces around London. It took place in surveillance-free zones at the edges or intersections of public and private spaces: at parish or county boundaries, just off the turnpike road, or in fields or clearings that were empty, undesirable and un-policed. 'The Fancy' – that uneasy alliance of royal and aristocratic amateurs, promoters, publicans, bookies, showmen and criminals

– would meet on the outer London commons of Bexley, Hornchurch, Smitham or Wimbledon; they would hide among the crowds at the Hounslow Races or the Barnet Horse Fair; or they would cross from Middlesex to Surrey or from Essex to Kent in small boats (from Hampton across to Moulsey Hurst, or down river to the Long Reach Tavern in the Erith Marshes). When a planned fight between Donovan and Hill on Streatham Common was stopped by the justices in 1825 it relocated to Mitcham Common. Prize Fights had a secret and particular geography with venues confirmed in particular London pubs just a few days in advance. When a London man fought a provincial then a mid-point would be chosen along the turnpike and 'the Fancy' would post through the night to arrive at dawn for the bout with carrier pigeons to be sent back to the bookies in London to confirm the result.

In 1823, the year before John Thurtell was hanged and anatomised, the writer William Hazlitt shared a coach with him along the Bath Road to Hungerford for the prize fight between Hickman, 'the Gas Man' from Bristol and the Cockney Bill Neate. Thurtell had boxed a little as a young man and on the tedious journey through a December day and night, he regaled Hazlitt some of his top tips: "Abstinence and exercise repeated alternately and without end... A yolk of an egg with a spoonful of rum in it is the first thing in a morning, and then a walk of six miles till breakfast." The coach only went as far as Newbury and they had to walk on in to Hungerford with the dawn. There at a roped-out ring in the grass by the 66th milestone the London crowd met Hickman's supporters who had come here from Bristol, Oxford and Gloucester. The rural stupid stood and gawped at the 'cits' who stared in turn and in fascination at Neate's slow attrition of the Gas Man, making a 'red ruin of the side of his face'. When it was over there was a race for the coaches back to town to deliver copy, Pierce Egan writing it up for the *Weekly Dispatch*, Hazlitt for The *Monthly Magazine*.

Washington Irving, visiting London from the United States, was amazed by prize-fighting's "chain of easy communication extending down from the peer to the pickpocket, through the medium of which a man of rank may find he has shaken hands at three removes, with the murderer on the gibbet." Hazlitt, the metropolitan man of letters, squeezed tandem in the mail coach with Thutell, the soon-to be-anatomised amateur of the prize ring, nicely illustrates the point.

*The Whitgift Almshouses, Croydon*

The fight promoters gravitated to locations beside gallows and gibbets (Smitham Bottom, Wimbledon Common, Kennington or Hounslow Heath). This was partly because in these unmapped spaces the gallows could serve as a signpost to the venue; partly too because for their prize fights they were seeking out those ambiguous spaces where the awful and the unlawful could overlap. The crowds for a hanging and for a bare-knuckle fight had much in common: they came for the adrenaline rush of the spectacle and for the circus rather than the bread. In 1792, in the final decade of the Kennington gallows, a black boxer called Mungo defeated a local Newington carpenter on Kennington Common. The Thomas A'Beckett pub with its upstairs ring where Henry Cooper and a host of other South London fighters learnt their craft was built over the site of the medieval Southwark gallows that had stood by the bridge at St Thomas Watering on the Old Kent Road.

Slowly all this *grand guignol* was tidied away. The traitors' spikes were taken down from above Temple Bar and the open-air gallows of Tyburn and Kennington withdrew behind prison walls. The civilising legislation of the 1814 Treason Act now insisted that traitors should only be beheaded once they were completely dead and in 1828 the Murder act was repealed. In the same way that regulated boxing stifled and replaced prize fighting so the Anatomy Act removed the market for grave robbery and the justifications for public dissection. By a fine irony it was the 'Burkers' Bishop and Williams - hanged in 1831 for killing a man and selling on his body to a surgeon and his teeth to a dentist – who were the last to undergo that very public evisceration. From now on surgeons had an alternative and limitless supply of pauper, convict and lunatic corpses for their anatomy lessons. The gibbet went a year later in 1832. 'Hanging in chains' was found to be indecorous, partly because King William was finding the coach journey from Clarence House out to Windsor past the dissipating remains on Hounslow Heath too distressing.

Just occasionally the old place names, like flesh on gibbeted bones, cling in the act of falling away. Jerry Abershaw fell into dust, but 'Jerry's Hill' is still there on Wimbledon Common. Mostly though the Gallows Greens and Hangman's Acres have made their excuses and departed. 'Jack Gutteridge's Gate' at the summit of Brixton Hill is no longer spoken of. At Smitham Bottom in 1838, The Times carried an auction notice for a "valuable parcel of meadow land known as Gibbet's Green, adjoining the high turnpike road from Croydon to Brighton" for building on. Later in the century after the railway arrived and abbreviated it, the place shrank down to mere Smitham. Even that foreshortening is now lost for in 2011 the station was renamed Coulsdon Town. "This sort of simple change", according to Croydon's cabinet member for planning, "can really help to build pride and confidence in an area"... local people found the new name "more fitting for the twenty-first century."

As a footnote to our journey we return to Croydon later that summer. We go back to that improbable high street survivor, the Whitgift alms houses, in the midst of its oubliette of a town centre in search of another and different version of death on the Brighton Road. Entering through its low narrow gateway is like stepping into the court of some minor and impecunious Oxbridge college. The flower beds, a simple geometry of lavender and begonia offset with clumps of red and white Through-the-Looking-Glass roses, are a delight. An armillary sphere on a pillar in the centre draws the eye and lines of worn wooden benches hug the four dark-brown mortar-lined walls of the court. The residents are out of sight, taking a Tudor siesta behind the tiled and hipped porches which lead to their separate chambers. Each one, supported by a pair of wooden brackets out of Hogarth's Gin Lane, hints at the arm of a gallows.

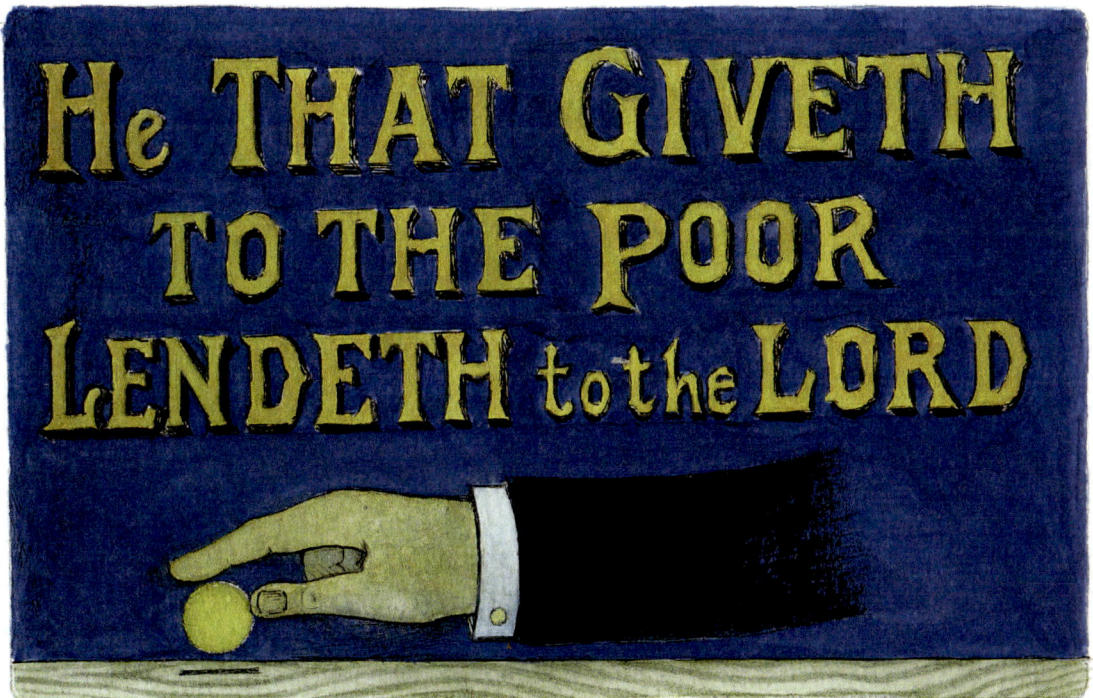

High brick chimneys are at each corner, but the town peers in over the top of them, higher still. The stone facings of Allders department store and the concrete and glass of more distant and yet more overtopping towers look down and in. Dave is chatting to the girl from the Clerk's office who has just let us in. She was going outside for lunch but now seems in no hurry. "I don't like to go out there, to be honest". She points through the tunnelled arch we have just entered by to the flash of suddenly distant shop-fronts.

If the garden is a delightful yet absurd survival in Croydon town centre then the chapel which we have arranged to visit overwhelms with its über-calm. We pass under a low arch into the cool of white distempered walls pierced by deep narrow windows above dark oak wainscoting. Twenty chairs and some older elm pews face the communion table's discreet crucifix and candlesticks; there is a vase of white lilies to one side. The lattice window behind the altar is screened by net curtain, adding another layer of whiteness and distance to the light that filters through. A woman outside in the street pauses and leans against the sill to light her cigarette, her back presses dark and suddenly sharply focused against the glass and I catch the brief spark of the lighter. The scrape and trill of a passing tram comes faintly through the wall. It is ringing its bell as it slows to negotiate the curve from George Street into Church Street, clanking Croydon's shoppers back home to Elmers End.

It was a passing reference to a memento mori that has brought us back here. A nineteenth century account records that a curious carved relief used to be displayed on the chapel wall, "a representation of Death as a skeleton digging a grave". I had phoned the alms houses to arrange to visit and asked them if Death was still there on the wall. I was passed on to the Whitgift's archivist who said he needed to check and went off to search his documents. A

week later he called back having drawn a blank but suggested I should come and see for myself. Scanning the chapel walls the portraits of John Whitgift and his niece are still to be seen in their frames, glowering charitably. "He that giveth to the poor lendeth to the Lord" runs the text. Their white lawn sleeves and ruffs look fitting. But the skeleton of Death has been tidied away and nobody knows what has become of it.

John Whitgift had been Elizabeth's trusty for twenty years. She called him teasingly 'my little black husband' and he was there for her at her deathbed, offering consolatory prayers, deferring his own departure until the following year. In 1604, chilled by Thames river mist, dead in his Lambeth palace of the marsh ague, borne over Brixton Hill and buried in Croydon, he came to his own particular South London requiem. As Archbishop of Canterbury he had been an enthusiastic procurer of others' too. Of the 'Forty Catholic Martyrs of England and Wales', fourteen lost their limbs and lights to the hangman's knife under his arch-episcopacy. The burnings at Smithfield had all but ceased so it was to Tyburn that most were dragged on their sleds to be hung and then to be dismembered upon the city's gates.

Rather than Catholics, Whitgift burnt books. In 1599 his 'Bishops' Ban' censored the works of Thomas Nashe (newly fallen from favour, having previously written a masque for Whitgift that was performed at his Croydon palace but five years earlier), translations of Tasso, works by Middleton and Marston and, for its erotic content, Marlowe's translation of Ovid's Amores. In what was the largest and most dramatic of Elizabeth's acts of censorship, the common hangman piled up these editions outside Stationer's Hall and burnt them: Pierce Penniless with his mouth full of ashes; Corinna of the long loose gown and the white neck, charred black.

I notice that the almswomen are still using the Book of Common Prayer for their services and I read the opening address of the order for Compline, "The Lord almighty grant us a quiet night and a perfect end". Their aged predecessors shivering in the draughty chapel would have looked up from their prayer books to that now vanished vanitas mundi on the wall as the minister rattled through the evening service, numbering off the skeleton's ribs as they waited for him to finish so that they could return to the relative warmth of their beds.

For the anatomised of Thornton Heath and the unburied of Smitham Bottom, Whitgift's bony sexton represented the unattainable 'decent' burial which had been denied them. Once held and tried under the Murder Act they would never escape its very prescriptive horror. Their companions on the gallows would be cut down and buried in the clean and forgetful earth. But for those marked by its "peculiar infamy" there remained a posting in perpetuity, to become a Thurtell in a glass case, bleached and wired to a bony whiteness, or an Abershaw in scarecrow suspension with the gibbet's screw biting deep into the skull. Death the skeleton had dug the graves for all the rest but for this elect there remained a slow unfinished dance. Outside, along the Brighton Road and down the Purley Way, comminuted to bone fragment, pulverised to road dust and homeopathic in their dilution, the ungrateful dead still blow between the passing cars, the trams and the goal posts.